# Apress Pocket Guides

*Apress Pocket Guides* present concise summaries of cutting-edge developments and working practices throughout the tech industry. Shorter in length, books in this series aim to deliver quick-to-read guides that are easy to absorb, perfect for the time-poor professional.

This series covers the full spectrum of topics relevant to the modern industry, from security, AI, machine learning, cloud computing, web development, product design, to programming techniques and business topics too.

Typical topics might include:

- A concise guide to a particular topic, method, function or framework

- Professional best practices and industry trends

- A snapshot of a hot or emerging topic

- Industry case studies

- Concise presentations of core concepts suited for students and those interested in entering the tech industry

- Short reference guides outlining 'need-to-know' concepts and practices.

More information about this series at https://link.springer.com/bookseries/17385.

# Web Forms with React

## Build Robust and Scalable Forms with React Hook Form

Usman Abdur Rehman

Apress®

*Web Forms with React: Build Robust and Scalable Forms with React Hook Form*

Usman Abdur Rehman
Islamabad, Pakistan

ISBN-13 (pbk): 979-8-8688-1223-1           ISBN-13 (electronic): 979-8-8688-1224-8
https://doi.org/10.1007/979-8-8688-1224-8

Managing Director, Apress Media LLC: Welmoed Spahr
Acquisitions Editor: James Robinson-Prior
Development Editor: James Markham
Editorial Assistant: Gryffin Winkler

Cover designed by eStudioCalamar

Distributed to the book trade worldwide by Springer Science+Business Media New York, 1 New York Plaza, Suite 4600, New York, NY 10004-1562, USA. Phone 1-800-SPRINGER, fax (201) 348-4505, e-mail orders-ny@springer-sbm.com, or visit www.springeronline.com. Apress Media, LLC is a California LLC and the sole member (owner) is Springer Science + Business Media Finance Inc (SSBM Finance Inc). SSBM Finance Inc is a **Delaware** corporation.

For information on translations, please e-mail booktranslations@springernature.com; for reprint, paperback, or audio rights, please e-mail bookpermissions@springernature.com.

Apress titles may be purchased in bulk for academic, corporate, or promotional use. eBook versions and licenses are also available for most titles. For more information, reference our Print and eBook Bulk Sales web page at http://www.apress.com/bulk-sales.

Any source code or other supplementary material referenced by the author in this book is available to readers on GitHub. For more detailed information, please visit https://www.apress.com/gp/services/source-code.

If disposing of this product, please recycle the paper

*Dedicated to my awesome mother, Waqarunnisa.*

# Table of Contents

# About the Author

**Usman Abdur Rehman** is a frontend tech lead for a US-based healthcare company with over four years of professional experience. As a self-taught developer, Usman studied everything related to programming from YouTube videos, tutorials, blogs, and books. Since gaining his first developer role, Usman has been motivated to give back to the community by teaching coding.

# About the Technical Reviewer

**Alexandru Tepes** is a full-time software engineer with a love for technology and health. He enjoys sharing what he's learned, reaching over 50,000 views on Medium with his simple and practical insights. Passionate about making complex ideas easy to understand, Alexandru writes about software, healthy living, and the ways these worlds connect. His goal is to help and inspire others to grow, learn, and improve their lives. When not working on software or writing, Alex explores how technology can enhance everyday experiences. This book is part of his journey to share knowledge and make a positive impact.

# Introduction

*Web Forms with React* is a succinct and practical guide to building robust, scalable, and reusable forms in React. Forms are an integral part of any software and are the source of data we see entered on the Web. From social media posts to selling products on ecommerce sites to YouTube videos and blog posts, most of the information on the Web is present because of the data that was entered through forms. It is therefore vital that we know how to properly handle forms, how to properly scale them, how to handle validations, etc. This book is a one-stop guide to setting up web forms from scratch using one of the most popular and robust frontend frameworks in use today, React Hook Form.

Standards and best practices are vital for everything we do, and a proper standard should be set in place so that everyone does the same thing and everyone is aware of the pros/cons of whatever might occur while adopting that practice. Forms in React can be handled in a hundred different ways, and this book proposes to set the standard on how to handle and set up forms using React. Once standards are in place, developers will be able to code robust, bug-free forms because they know they are making forms that are being used by millions of developers and if they run into issues they would be able to find solutions to those issues pretty easily.

It is also important that scalability is kept in mind while making any software feature, whether it's a server function, a UI component, or something else. React Hook Form makes sure that the forms are not only performant but also scalable. Most of the time, a certain part of a form gets repeated across an application. For example, the email and password fields are often present in the Signin, Signup, and Edit Profile sections, and they have a similar set of validations, constraints, etc. So we will look at how to handle these so they can be reused across the application where they are required.

Validations are always important whether they are server-side or client-side validations. React Hook Form provides a nice interface for hooking up validations by either using normal HTML validation or using a third-party validation library like Yup, Zod, etc.

By the end of this book, you will have the knowledge and confidence to build strong and reusable web forms from the ground up.

**CHAPTER 1**

# Forms in React

Forms are an integral part of any software including the Web and are the way of data entry for all the user data you see on the Web. From social media posts to ecommerce products to YouTube videos/blog posts, most data on the Web is present because of the data that was entered through forms. It is therefore vital that you know how to properly handle forms, how to properly scale them, how to handle validations for them, etc.

This chapter talks about the usual approach taken by novice developers for handling forms in React and the cons of it.

## Native Form Handling

Working with forms requires a lot of different steps from handling state to validation to making sure the form is robust, scalable, and reusable. I would go through every step to see how native React handles all these and what are the cons related to them.

## Handling State

Listing 1-1 shows you what a traditional form looks like with native state handling (using useState).

© Usman Abdur Rehman 2025
U. A. Rehman, *Web Forms with React*, Apress Pocket Guides,
https://doi.org/10.1007/979-8-8688-1224-8_1

*Listing 1-1.* The traditional way of handling state

```
import { useState } from "react";
export const HandlingState = () => {
  const [name, setName] = useState("");
  return (
    <form>
      <input value={name} onChange={(e) => setName(e.target.
      value)} />
    </form>
  );
};
```

What should you do in the case when there are multiple fields in a form? Should you use two states for those two fields or one object state that handles the state for the whole form? There is no standard for it.

Also, this traditional way of performing state update triggers rerenders on every keystroke and can be disastrous if you have a large form that hasn't been memoized properly.

## Handling Validation

Listing 1-2 shows you how traditional validation is performed in forms.

*Listing 1-2.* The traditional way of handling validation

```
import { useState } from "react";

export const HandlingValidation = () => {
  const [name, setName] = useState("");
  const [error, setError] = useState("");
  return (
    <form>
      <input
```

```
      value={name}
      onChange={(e) => setName(e.target.value)}
        onBlur={(e) => {
        if (!e.target.value) setError("The name is
        required");
        else setError("");
      }}
    />
    {error && <p>{error}</p>}
  </form>
);
};
```

Again, there is no standard for validating forms natively. Maybe there is a requirement for handling validations on change, focus, or form submission; the way the validation is applied could differ depending on which scenario it is.

Also let's say you want to apply a complex validation use case where you want that if a field is visited (touched) and the validation fails on change, then the related validation error should be shown. The inclusion of more states and conditions for handling cases like these could introduce bugs in the form.

There is a need for a clear-cut standard for doing validations.

## Standard

As discussed in the previous two sections, there is no standard for performing validations, handling state, or making a form in React. When that is the case, there is a high chance every developer on your team would use a different strategy to make forms. Since everything can be done in a million different ways, every person on the team would use their strategy to implement a certain feature, which, when the feature would be worked on again in the future, to fix a bug or to add an enhancement, would not present an ideal solution since not everyone is familiar with that strategy the developer used to code the feature.

## Learning

Even if you have a particular custom form-making strategy/standard in your company, if you get stuck somewhere, the only way to get through that is to consult your team members. There would be no resources on the Internet regarding learning it or fixing bugs if you ever encounter one.

## Scalability and Reusability

If you make a form using native state handling and custom validation logic, it will not scale properly.

The first reason for that is performance. If you make a form in React using no widely used/accepted standard, there is a chance it has some performance flaws in it, which would hurt you in the longer run once you start using these methodologies to make bigger forms.

The second reason for that is reusability. You would be able to scale better if you could make easy-to-use, reusable form components out of an existing form. The crux of React or any other modern framework is reusability, and if you can't do that, then any development approach would not work.

## Robustness

Each and every part of your web application must be robust and not error-prone. Using a nonstandard way of making forms won't help achieve that objective.

# The Solution

The solution for every con that we face as described above is using a library that is used by millions of developers around the world. Using a library gives us the following advantages:

1.  You would have a standard for building forms, and that standard would be easily adaptable and learnable by developers who would be joining your team. Following a standard would ensure there would be a certain set of practices that would be used by developers in your team so the chances of something going wrong would be minimal as well.

2.  This would ensure that the application you are building is robust since a library with millions of downloads, hundreds of issue resolutions, etc. is ideally bug-free and has been through the rigorous cycle of development that every software practice goes through.

3.  Scalability/reusability would be available out of the box since it would ensure that you are using one of the best strategies, if not the best strategy, for building forms both performance- and coding-wise.

4.  It would have a developer-friendly API so you will be able to solve complex issues while using minimal code and would be able to focus on building vital features of your application without worrying about the standard, robustness, etc. of your form code.

# Summary

In this chapter we discussed the current form-making strategies in React in detail and why it is not recommended to make forms that way.

In the next chapter, we will take a look at a very popular and widely used React form library, *React Hook Form*, and we will see how it addresses all our concerns that we discussed in this chapter.

# CHAPTER 2

# React Hook Form

In the last chapter, we looked at the cons of using our custom approaches
to manage form actions like state management, validations, etc. We
saw how using traditional ways of building forms can make our forms
less robust and scalable and how not following a standard brings
nonuniformity to your application.

In this chapter, we will discuss React Hook Form, a library that is being
used by millions of developers to make performant and robust forms. We
will take a look at why I chose this library and what it brings to the table.

## Why React Hook Form?

While searching for that one React form library, I stumbled upon a lot
of different options, some of which I had used in a professional capacity
before as well. React Hook Form checked a lot of boxes and was so far the
best choice compared with the other options like Formik, Redux Form, etc.

In this section, we will take a look at why you as a React developer
should consider building your forms using this library and how React
Hook Form is comparatively better than other React form libraries like
Formik and Redux Form.

© Usman Abdur Rehman 2025
U. A. Rehman, *Web Forms with React*, Apress Pocket Guides,
https://doi.org/10.1007/979-8-8688-1224-8_2

# Performance

React state on every update rerenders the whole component, which means every calculation and subcomponent would be recalculated and rerendered if not properly memoized.

Normal React form libraries like Formik use React state for managing field values, which means that for every keystroke in an input field, for example, you are rerendering the whole form, which should not be the case but that is how state works. This results in a decrease in performance as the form size increases if the sub-form components are not properly memoized.

React Hook Form on the other hand uses refs to manage form values. Every input component in your form in React Hook Form is an uncontrolled component. If you type in an input field in React Hook Form, it does not trigger any rerender and only keeps track of the form values using refs, which makes it much faster than other form libraries.

Also because React Hook Form has uncontrolled form components, there is less overhead, and components mount very quickly.

# GitHub Stats

The GitHub stats of any library dictate a lot regarding whether that library is popular in the developer community, whether its maintenance has stopped or not, whether it's being worked on frequently or not, etc. In this section, we will take a look at some of these GitHub stats, which dictate that React Hook Form is the best form library for React.

GitHub stars serve as a measure of a library's popularity, quality, and likeness. A developer is most likely to use a library with more stars. At the time of writing, React Hook Form has 39.1k GitHub stars as opposed to the 33.4k GitHub stars of Formik.

React Hook Form is maintained at a regular interval. Whenever you open its GitHub page, you will see that the latest commit was made almost one to two days ago, which means it's being currently worked on for either bug/issue fixes or new features and improvements. Its counterparts, Formik and Redux Form, have the last commits from last year, which speaks about the level of maintenance they receive.

The number of GitHub issues for React Hook Form at the time of this writing is 1. This means it's a robust library and doesn't get a lot of issues reported or even if issues are reported, they are being dealt with by the team as quickly as possible. However, for Formik and Redux Form at the time of this writing, they have 690 and 475 open issues, respectively, and a large portion of them are bugs.

For React Hook Form, the number of open pull requests (PRs) is very low because the pull request merge ratio is very high. For Formik the number of open pull requests is very high, which means it is not being maintained by its developers. For Redux Form, the open pull requests are from 2023 meaning not a lot of people are actively using this library. You can check out the GitHub stats for React Hook Form and Formik in Figure 2-1.

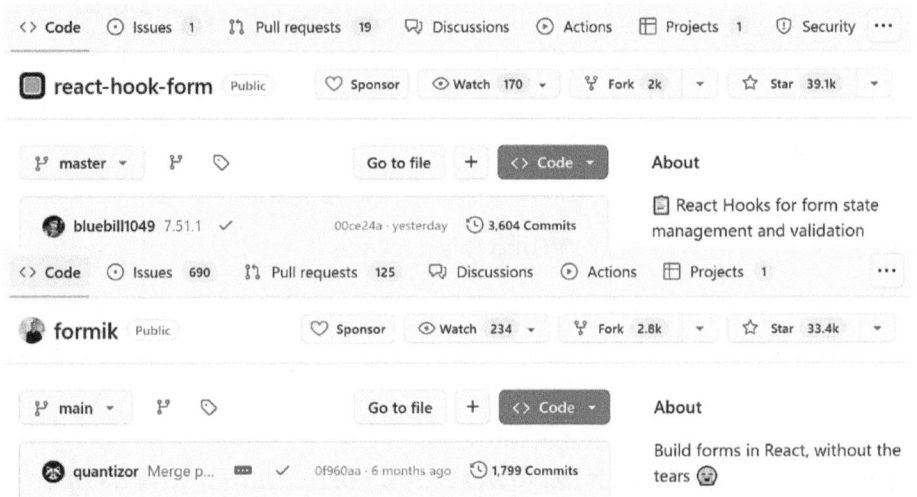

***Figure 2-1.*** *GitHub stats for React Hook Form and Formik*

# npm Installs

React Hook Form slowly and gradually is becoming the most used React form library out there. As a reference, in April 2023, both Formik and React Hook Form had almost similar downloads (around 2 million). However, at the time of this writing, React Hook Form has double the downloads (around 5 million) than those of Formik (around 2.7 million) as depicted in Figure 2-2.

It should be good practice to use a library that is the most popular/used because it helps with a variety of things. The most popular library would have the most learning material and Stack Overflow questions on the Internet meaning developers would be up and running in no time.

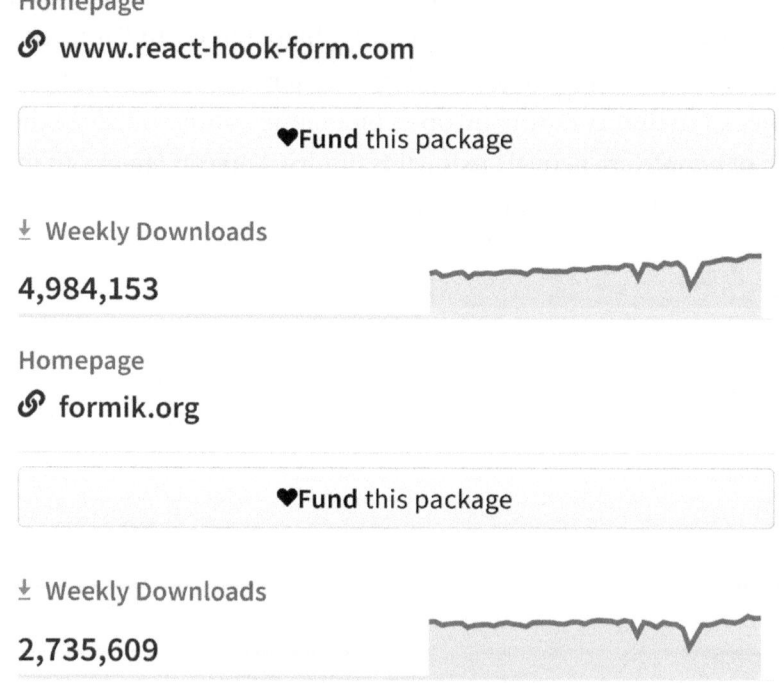

**Figure 2-2.** *npm installs for React Hook Form and Formik as of March 17, 2024*

# Type Safety

React Hook Form is built in TypeScript, so it provides end-to-end type safety for everything. If we specify a type object for our form values, every function or value given to us by React Hook Form for that form would adhere to that type signature.

As you can see in Figure 2-3, a type `FormData` has been defined with two properties `firstName` and `lastName`, both having a type of string. Because of that when a string param is passed in the `setValue` function alongside the `lastName` key, TypeScript does not give any error. However, TypeScript does throw an error when the wrong type is used with the `firstName` key in the `setValue` function (Boolean) as well as when we try to access a property `bill` that doesn't belong in the `FormData` type we passed in the form.

You don't have to worry about what `setValue` and `errors` are. We will take a detailed look at them in the next chapters.

```
type FormData = {
  firstName: string
  lastName: string
}

<button
  type="button"
  onClick={() => {
    setValue("lastName", "luo") // ✅
    setValue("firstName", true) // ✗: true is not string
    errors.bill // ✗: property bill does not exist
  }}
>
  SetValue
</button>
```

***Figure 2-3.*** *TypeScript giving errors on wrong field names + value types*

# Zero Dependencies

React Hook Form has 0 third-party dependencies. Normally libraries like Formik have tons of third-party dependencies. The problem with having third-party dependencies is that if one of them has a bug, this could introduce a bug in the dependent library as well. This makes React Hook Form more robust than its counterparts. Also, the installation time + module size would be much less since no third-party libraries would be installed along with it.

# Validation

React Hook Form has a variety of ways to validate your form state. You can validate your inputs using HTML5 validation; popular third-party validation libraries like Yup, Joi, Zod, etc.; and custom validation solutions. Also, along with that, you have diverse options of validation strategies like applying validation on change, blur, touched, submit, or all as well as the ability to choose revalidation strategies.

Formik on the other hand can validate using custom validation solutions or Yup only. Even if you want to apply some easy validations like required, min, max, etc., without any third-party library, you will have to write JavaScript code for it, and you can't use a simple solution like passing an object with required, min, and max properties and so on.

# Subscriptions

React Hook Form provides you with the ability to subscribe to individual input state changes without the need to rerender the entire form on state change. Normally if you want to monitor any state change, you need to have a useEffect that runs on state change. That means that you must have a state for every input, which changes on every keystroke (like in Formik and others).

Even though React Hook Form has uncontrolled React form components (using refs), it still gives us the ability to subscribe to individual field state changes, which makes it very powerful.

This has been explained in a brilliant way in Figure 2-4. The four checkboxes can be considered as four individual child components of the form. Components 1 and 3 are subscribed to the input field, so whenever any value of that field would change, these components would rerender and get the updated value, which can be used by them to do anything like make a query to the backend, show or hide something, etc. Components 2 and 4 however are not subscribed to the input field (these components are not concerned with the input field's data), so they would not rerender at all. This is what makes React Hook Form a performant library.

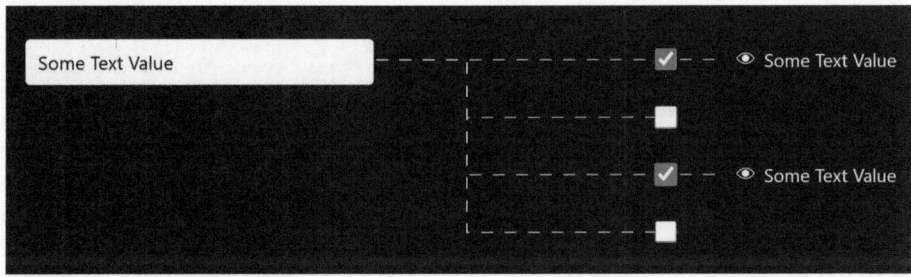

***Figure 2-4.*** *A figure showing field subscriptions in individual components in action*

## Cross-Platform

React Hook Form is available for both mobile and web (React Native and React). A library for building forms for both major platforms with the same API is a pretty cool thing to have in your arsenal.

# Dev Tools

React Hook Form has amazing dev tools as depicted in Figure 2-5, which can be used to monitor state changes related to the form fields. It also can scroll to that exact input if that input's label is clicked in the dev tools. It can help debug our form state without the need to add logging statements everywhere in our code.

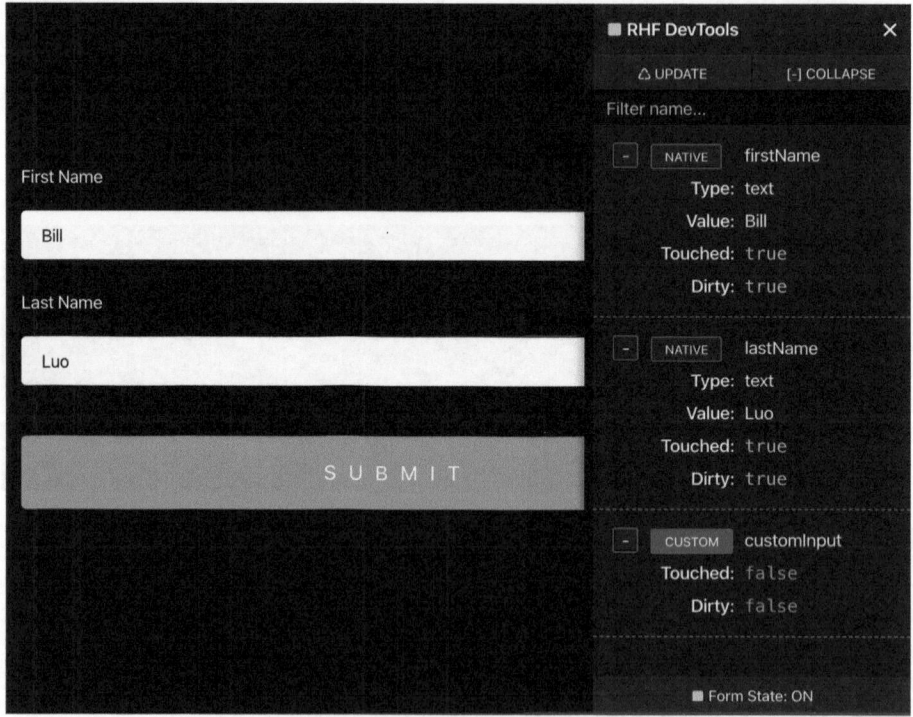

***Figure 2-5.*** *An example form built using React Hook Form and its dev tools*

# Form Builder

React Hook Form has an amazing form builder on its website. You can specify which inputs and their corresponding simple validations you want to add to your form, and it generates the code for it. If the form you are making is generic without any extra complicated functionality, you can use the form builder to make your form. It can also be used to make a boilerplate for your form so that you can add the other complicated stuff in that form builder–generated code.

# Features Comparison

All the features we discussed are summarized in Table 2-1.

***Table 2-1.*** *Features Comparison Between React Hook Form and Formik*

| Features | React Hook Form | Formik |
|---|---|---|
| Performance | Fast (refs) | Medium (state) |
| Type safety | Available for everything | Available but not for functions like setFieldValue, setFieldError, etc. |
| Validation | Built-in, Zod, Joi, Yup, Superstruct + custom | Yup + custom |
| npm downloads (at the time of writing) | Around 5 million | Around 2.7 million |
| GitHub stats (at the time of writing) | 39.1k GitHub stars<br>Few or no open PRs<br>Good issue resolution<br>Maintenance + continuous new version releases | 33.4k GitHub stars<br>Hundreds of open PRs<br>Bad issue resolution<br>No maintenance and new feature development |

*(continued)*

15

**Table 2-1.** (*continued*)

| Features | React Hook Form | Formik |
|---|---|---|
| Dependencies | 0 | 8 |
| Subscriptions | Ability to subscribe to individual inputs without rerendering the whole form | Ability to subscribe to individual inputs while rerendering the whole form |
| Dev tools | ✅ | ✖ |
| Form builder | ✅ | ✖ |

# Summary

In this chapter, we discussed the React Hook Form library and, via comparison with libraries like Formik and Redux Form, saw what features it brings to the table like performance, type safety, etc. and how it's better than the others.

In the next chapter, we will take a look at the basics of React Hook Form and even build a basic form by the end of that chapter.

# CHAPTER 3

# React Hook Form Basics

In the last chapter, I compared React Hook Form with other React form libraries like Formik and Redux Form and pointed out the differences these libraries had in terms of performance, implementation under the hood, popularity, support, etc.

In this chapter, I will discuss the basics of React Hook Form. You will look at some core API of this library to see how you can use it.

## The Core

The core of the React Hook Form library is the useForm hook. This hook returns everything you need to build your form, from refs for the input fields, which would be used to do validations, to individual change and blur handlers for the inputs, the submit handler for the form, validation errors, etc.

In this section, I will inspect the useForm hook in detail so that you can see what params it expects, what it returns, and how it works overall.

© Usman Abdur Rehman 2025
U. A. Rehman, *Web Forms with React*, Apress Pocket Guides,
https://doi.org/10.1007/979-8-8688-1224-8_3

# Basic Usage

Here is a basic example of how you would make a form using React Hook Form.

***Listing 3-1.*** Basic form built using React Hook Form

```
import { useForm, SubmitHandler } from "react-hook-form";
type Inputs = {
  name: string;
  email: string;
};
export const BasicForm = () => {
  const { register, handleSubmit } = useForm<Inputs>();

  const onSubmit: SubmitHandler<Inputs> = (data) => console.
  log(data);

  return (
    <form onSubmit={handleSubmit(onSubmit)}>
      <input placeholder="Name" {...register("name")} />
      <input placeholder="Email" {...register("email")} />
      <input type="submit" />
    </form>
  );
};
```

| Name | Email | Submit |

***Figure 3-1.*** *An example form built using React Hook Form*

In this example form as can be seen in Figure 3-1. there are two input fields Name and Email. I have used the `register` and `handleSubmit` functions returned from the `useForm` hook to handle this form. The `register` and `handleSubmit` functions would be used for form state management and form submission, respectively. These functions would be explained in detail in their respective sections later in this chapter.

# Using TypeScript

As mentioned in the previous chapter, React Hook Form is a TypeScript-compatible library, which means that you should use types with it to garner its full power. You can see in the start of Listing 3-1 that there is a type `Inputs` with two properties `name` and `email` both having a type of string. These two type properties indicate that there are two input fields in this form that expect a type string as their value (text field).

Then that type has been passed in the `useForm` hook as a type generic. This ensures that whichever property or function you would use from the `useForm` hook, it would adhere to the type you provided + would provide auto completions for object properties, which have to correspond to the type property names in the type passed in the `useForm` hook. Furthermore, if you would use any field key not present in the type passed in the `useForm` hook, you would get a TypeScript error, which would be good for developing robust forms.

You can also not pass any type to the `useForm` hook if you are using JavaScript or if you don't want to. Passing types in `useForm` is not mandatory. However, I would recommend you use types with React Hook Form to get appropriate linting/auto completions/errors in your IDE/text editor.

# useForm Returned Values

In the most basic implementation, the useForm hook can be used without passing it any param. As shown in the example above, it gives us some useful objects and functions that we can use to make our form. Let's go over them one by one.

## register

*Listing 3-2.* The register function

```
const { onChange, onBlur, name, ref } = register("firstName");
```

The register function as you can see in Listing 3-2, is one of the core functions returned by the useForm hook. This function powers every input field in the form. A string key has to be passed to this function as a param, which should be unique to the form. The register function when called returns the corresponding onChange, onBlur, name, and ref for the respective field.

This ref is the key to how React Hook Form behaves. The whole point of React Hook Form is that it is more performant than other libraries, and using refs is the reason that is. As discussed in the previous chapter, React Hook Form does data management of the form using refs and not state. This ref returned by the register function is responsible for writing the data to the fields if some initial values are provided to the useForm hook plus getting the data in the onSubmit function and so on (more details on this in a later section).

The onChange and onBlur functions and the name string are responsible for keeping track of the data that is being entered and, in turn, do various operations like applying validation for that data (on change or on blur). You will look at validations in more detail in Chapter 5. The name string has the same string value that we pass to the register function.

This `register` function also takes in an object as a second param, which is optional where you can supply basic native validation rules like if the field should be required, the field should have a certain length constraint and so on (more on this in future chapters).

## handleSubmit

***Listing 3-3.*** The handleSubmit function

```
<form onSubmit={handleSubmit(onSubmit)}></form>
```

`handleSubmit` as can be seen in Listing 3-3, is just a wrapper for the `onSubmit` function we pass to the `onSubmit` prop of the `form` component. This function only gets the form data when validations are successful. Once the submit button is clicked, the validations (if any) would be applied. If all validations are successful, this `onSubmit` function would be called with the data of the form as a param; otherwise, it would not be called and validation errors would be populated in the `formState` (discussed in a later section). The function passed in the `handleSubmit` function can be either synchronous or asynchronous.

## watch

***Listing 3-4.*** The watch function

```
watch("name");
watch(["name", "email"]);
```

This function would watch for field value changes. This function expects a string value or values (as an array) as a param (as can be seen in Listing 3-4), which should coincide with any of the field names. If any of the fields corresponding to the field names passed in the `watch` function would change, then the entire form would rerender, and you would be able to do anything you want to do based on those field changes (e.g., using a useEffect to fetch new records based on a value change in a dropdown in your form); otherwise, the component would not rerender at all because of the ref model that React Hook Form is based on.

This is awesome since you can only decide to rerender the form component for specific input changes and not all input changes (like in Formik as discussed in Chapter 2), which boosts the performance of your forms.

If you want to rerender only a child component based on a field change, then a better way to go about this would be to use the useWatch hook. I will discuss this in a future chapter.

## formState

*Listing 3-5.* The formState object

```
const { errors, isLoading, isValid, ...rest } = formState;
```

formState is an object that contains information regarding the state in which the form is as can be seen in Listing 3-5. This object contains the current errors, current field names that have been touched (fields that have been focused and blurred at least once), the state of the form (is loading, has been edited, has been submitted successfully, is validating), etc.

You can use this info to do certain things on the UI like display errors, disable the submit button if any form field hasn't been touched or if any form field has no new data entered, display a loader while the form is submitting, etc. The possibilities are endless.

## reset

The reset function can be used to reset the entire form state to whatever was originally specified as initial values (via the defaultValues param) in the useForm hook. If nothing was supplied in the defaultValues param, then this function would empty all the fields.

The reset function also takes in an optional param. If you want that the form's state resets to something other than the defaultValues, you can pass that object to the reset function as a param.

## useForm Params

The useForm hook also expects some params, and they can be divided into two categories: form value–related params and validation-related params. We are going to look at validation in detail in Chapter 5. For now, let's just only discuss the form value params.

## defaultValues

***Listing 3-6.*** The defaultValues param

```
useForm({
    defaultValues: {
      firstName: '',
      lastName: ''
    }
  })

useForm({
  defaultValues: async () => fetch('/api-endpoint');
})
```

The defaultValues param is used to populate the initial data of a form. It expects either an object conforming with the type signature passed to the useForm hook or an async function that would return an object (an async function fetching initial values from a backend) conforming with that particular type signature as can be seen in Listing 3-6.

## values

*Listing 3-7.* The values param

```
useForm({
    values: {
       firstName: '',
       lastName: ''
    }
  })
```

This param as can be seen in Listing 3-7, will react to changes, and every time this param would change, the useForm hook would forward this change to the entire form. This param is useful when you want to change your form state based on some external change like a prop value being passed from another component, some global state, or some query data coming from a library that works with hooks (TanStack Query).

# Summary

In this chapter, we looked at the basics of how React Hook Form works. We explored the core of React Hook Form, the useForm hook. We looked at a basic example form, built using that hook, and explored its API.

In this next chapter, we will dive into React Hook Form a bit more by actually building some forms with React Hook Form.

**CHAPTER 4**

# Making Forms with React Hook Form

In the last chapter, I discussed the core of React Hook Form, the useForm hook. I discussed how you can use the useForm hook to make a basic form and what each object and function returned by the useForm hook is for.

In this chapter, I will make a couple of forms using React Hook Form. I would first describe what I want to build, and then I will build those forms step by step using React Hook Form so that you can understand it thoroughly.

## BMI Calculator

In this section, I will develop a BMI calculator. This form would have the following salient features:

- A form with two number fields, height and weight.

- The height and weight fields would be required since both of those values are required to calculate the BMI. The respective validation errors, for example, height is required, and so on would be shown below each field when validation would be performed.

© Usman Abdur Rehman 2025
U. A. Rehman, *Web Forms with React*, Apress Pocket Guides,
https://doi.org/10.1007/979-8-8688-1224-8_4

- Upon form submission, the BMI would be calculated based on the formula Weight in kilograms/(Height in meters)$^2$, which would then be shown alongside the submit button.

First of all, I will write the HTML for the form. It would contain a React component that would return a form tag with two input fields and a submit button inside as seen in Listing 4-1.

***Listing 4-1.*** HTML skeleton for the BMI calculator

```
export default function BMI() {
  return (
    <form>
      <input type="number" placeholder="Height (in meters)"
      step="any" />
      <input type="number" placeholder="Weight (in kg)"
      step="any" />
      <div />
      <div className="footer">
        <button type="submit">Calculate</button>
        <p className="result">BMI:</p>
      </div>
    </form>
  );
}
```

Styling is not our priority, but I will still apply some basic styles to it as can be seen in Listing 4-2.

***Listing 4-2.*** CSS styles for the BMI form

```css
input {
  margin-bottom: 10px;
  padding: 12px;
  border-radius: 4px;
  border: 1px solid black;
  display: block;
}

p {
  margin: 0;
}

.error {
  margin-bottom: 5px;
  color: red;
  font-size: 14px;
}

.footer {
  display: flex;
  align-items: center;
  gap: 12px;
}

.result {
  font-size: 14px;
}
```

The form would look something like Figure 4-1.

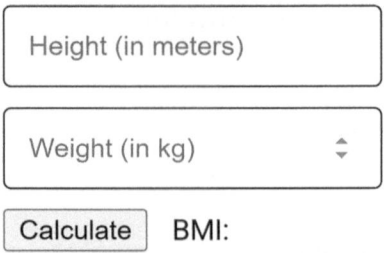

*Figure 4-1.* *BMI calculator form*

Let's start adding code related to React Hook Form to our form. First of all, I will define the type for the useForm hook as given in Listing 4-3. Since there are two fields in our form (height and weight) and both are of type number, the type for the form would look something like the following.

*Listing 4-3.* FormData type for useForm

```
interface FormData {
  height: number;
  weight: number;
}
```

I will then call the useForm hook inside the BMI component and pass the FormData type there as you can see in Listing 4-4.

*Listing 4-4.* Calling the useForm hook

```
import { useForm } from "react-hook-form";

export default function BMI() {
  const {
    register,
    handleSubmit,
    formState: { errors },
  } = useForm<FormData>();
```

As discussed in the previous chapter, the register function is key in the working of React Hook Form. The register function returns the onChange, onBlur, name, and ref for a specific field.

I would spread the register function in both fields as can be seen in Listing 4-5.

***Listing 4-5.*** Spreading the register function in input fields

```
<input
      type="number"
      {...register("height", { required: true, valueAsNumber:
      true })}
      placeholder="Height (in meters)"
      step="any"
   />

   <input
      type="number"
      {...register("weight", { required: true, valueAsNumber:
      true })}
      placeholder="Weight (in kg)"
      step="any"
   />
```

As you can see, in addition to the first param in the register function (field key), I have also passed an object as a second param with two key-value pairs, required:true and valueAsNumber:true.

The required property if true would add a validation in the form for that field where you won't be able to submit a form if there is no text entered in that particular field.

By default, any value inside an input text field would be a string value. However, I need number values for the text I would enter inside the height/weight fields. valueAsNumber:true would parse the value entered to a number, because of which I would get number values for height and weight inside the onSubmit function.

Now I would like to show the validation errors in the form. I would show the individual validation errors below each field. I would get the validation errors from the formState object, which is returned from the useForm hook as seen in Listing 4-4.

The errors variable would be an object. The key would be the field name, and the value would be an error object of the following type as can be seen in Listing 4-6.

**Listing 4-6.**  Shape of the error object

```
{
  message: string;
  type: string;
  ref: React.RefObject;
}
```

where the type property would have the value required in case of required validation. For this particular form, I will check if the errors object has a field key corresponding to the field (there is an error). Then I will check if the type property of that object has the value required. If that is so, I will show an error for the corresponding field below it as can be seen in Listing 4-7.

**Listing 4-7.**  Mapping the errors

```
<input
  type="number"
  {...register("height", { required: true, valueAsNumber:
  true })}
  placeholder="Height (in meters)"
  step="any"
/>
{errors.height?.type === "required" && (
  <p className="error">Height is required</p>
)}
```

```
<input
  type="number"
  {...register("weight", { required: true, valueAsNumber:
  true })}
  placeholder="Weight (in kg)"
  step="any"
/>
{errors.weight?.type === "required" && (
  <p className="error">Weight is required</p>
)}
```

Now I would add the onSubmit function for the form. I will pass in a handleSubmit function as a prop value to the onSubmit function of the form component with a custom onSubmit function as a param where I will write the code for form submission. This function would receive the form data, and I would use the formula I mentioned in the form description I provided to calculate the value.

After calculating the value, I will set a state, which I would display alongside the BMI label in the form footer as can be seen in Listing 4-8.

***Listing 4-8.*** The form submission logic

```
import { useState } from "react"
import { useForm, SubmitHandler } from "react-hook-form"
export default const BMI() {
  const [bmi, setBMI] = useState<string>();

  const onSubmit: SubmitHandler<FormData> = (data) => {
      const { height, weight } = data;
      const bmi = (weight / height ** 2).toFixed(1);
      setBMI(bmi);
  };

  return (
      <form onSubmit={handleSubmit(onSubmit)}>
```

31

If you now enter a valid height and weight like 3 meters and 50 kilograms and click the Calculate button, you will see the BMI 5.6 being shown alongside the BMI: label like in Figure 4-2.

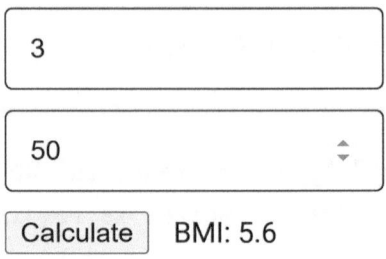

***Figure 4-2.*** *BMI value calculated from the BMI calculator*

And that is it. Just like that I was able to make a basic form using React Hook Form.

# Signup Form

In this section, I will build a Signup form. This form would have the following salient features:

- A form with four fields, first name, last name, email, and password.

- The first name, email, and password fields would be required. The email field would have an email pattern validation so that it only allows valid email to be entered in the text field. The password field would have a minimum length validation of at least ten characters so that the password is long. The respective validation errors, for example, the first name is required, and so on would be shown below each field when validation would be performed.

- Upon form submission, the form data would be sent to a dummy endpoint /signup.

- During submission the submit button text would change from Signup to Submitting .... During submission or when no input field has been modified, the submit button would be disabled.

- A third-party UI components library (Material UI) would be integrated.

The basic HTML structure of the form would look like the following as can be seen in Listing 4-9.

***Listing 4-9.*** HTML skeleton for the Signup form

```
export default function Signup() {
  return (
    <form>
      <div className="form-container">
        <div>
          <input placeholder="First name" />
        </div>
        <div>
          <input placeholder="Last name" />
        </div>
        <div>
          <input placeholder="Email" />
        </div>
        <div>
          <input placeholder="Password" />
        </div>
      </div>
```

```
      <button type="submit">Signup</button>
    </form>
  );
}
```

I will apply some basic styles as can be seen in Listing 4-10.

***Listing 4-10.*** CSS styles for the Signup form

```css
* {
  box-sizing: border-box;
}

.form-container {
  width: 400px;
  display: grid;
  grid-template-columns: 200px 200px;
  column-gap: 10px;
}

input {
  margin-bottom: 10px;
  padding: 12px;
  border-radius: 4px;
  border: 1px solid black;
  display: block;
  width: 100%;
}

.error {
  margin: 0;
  margin-bottom: 10px;
  color: red;
  font-size: 14px;
}
```

The form would look something like in Figure 4-3.

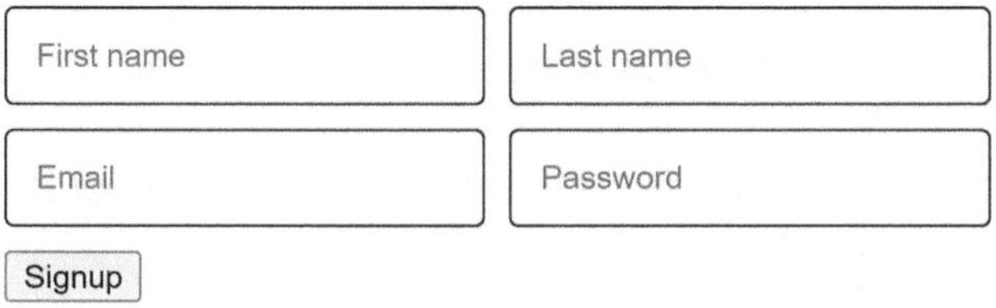

***Figure 4-3.*** *Signup form*

Now I will define the type for the useForm hook. Since I have four fields and all of them would be of type string, the type would look something like the following as can be seen in Listing 4-11.

***Listing 4-11.*** FormData type for the useForm hook

```
interface FormData {
  firstName: string;
  lastName: string;
  password: string;
  email: string;
}
```

I will then call the useForm hook and pass this type there as can be seen in Listing 4-12.

***Listing 4-12.*** Calling the useForm hook

```
import { useForm } from "react-hook-form";

export default function Signup() {
  const {
    register,
    handleSubmit,
    formState: { errors },
  } = useForm<FormData>();
```

Now I will spread the register function in all fields. Since I know that the first name, email, and password fields are required, I would add required:true in the register options object like in Listing 4-13.

***Listing 4-13.*** Spreading the register function in input fields

```
<div className="form-container">
  <div>
    <input
      {...register("firstName", { required: true })}
      placeholder="First name"
    />
  </div>
  <div>
    <input {...register("lastName")} placeholder="Last name" />
  </div>
  <div>
    <input
      {...register("email", {
        required: true,
      })}
      placeholder="Email"
    />
  </div>
  <div>
    <input
      {...register("password", {
        required: true,
      })}
      placeholder="Password"
    />
  </div>
</div>
```

Now I would like to add pattern matching validation to the email field. That can easily be done by passing a `pattern` property in the register options param, which would have a regex as a value. If the corresponding input value doesn't match with that regex, then a validation error would be added for the pattern.

The email regex would look something like the following as can be seen in Listing 4-14.

**Listing 4-14.**  Regex pattern for an email

```
/^[\w\-\.]+@([\w-]+\.)+[\w-]{2,4}$/
```

where

- `^[\w\-\.]+` would match the start of the string with word characters, -, and . one or more times.

- `@` would match the @ character.

- `([\w-]+\.)+` would match word characters one or more times. `\.` would match a dot.

- `[\w-]{2,4}$` would match the end of the string with word characters between lengths 2 and 4.

I would pass this pattern in the `pattern` property of register options as can be seen in Listing 4-15.

**Listing 4-15.**  Passing the pattern property in register options

```
<input
        {...register("email", {
          required: true,
          pattern: /^[\w-\.]+@([\w-]+\.)+[\w-]{2,4}$/,
        })}
        placeholder="Email"
    />
```

Similarly for password I want to add a minimum length validation. That can be done easily by passing the required length in the `minLength` property of the register options as can be seen in Listing 4-16.

***Listing 4-16.*** Passing the minLength property in register options

```
<input
        {...register("password", {
          required: true,
          minLength: 10,
        })}
        placeholder="Password"
      />
```

Let's map the errors. With required I was mapping the required errors only when type had a value required. Now for other error types like pattern, I would show the errors only when type would have a value pattern and so on. It would look something like Listing 4-17.

***Listing 4-17.*** Mapping the errors

```
<div className="form-container">
    <div>
        <input
          {...register("firstName", { required: true })}
          placeholder="First name"
        />
        {errors.firstName?.type === "required" && (
          <p className="error">First Name is required</p>
        )}
    </div>
    <div>
        <input {...register("lastName")} placeholder="Last
        name" />
```

```
      </div>
      <div>
        <input
          {...register("email", {
            required: true,
            pattern: /^[\w-\.]+@([\w-]+\.)+[\w-]{2,4}$/,
          })}
          placeholder="Email"
        />
        {errors.email?.type === "required" && (
          <p className="error">Email is required</p>
        )}
        {errors.email?.type === "pattern" && (
          <p className="error">Email is invalid</p>
        )}
      </div>
      <div>
        <input
          {...register("password", {
            required: true,
            minLength: 10,
          })}
          placeholder="Password"
        />
        {errors.password?.type === "required" && (
          <p className="error">Password is required</p>
        )}
        {errors.password?.type === "minLength" && (
          <p className="error">Password should have at least
          10 characters</p>
        )}
      </div>
    </div>
```

Now I would add the onSubmit functionality for the form. As discussed initially, I will send the form data to a dummy endpoint /signup as can be seen in Listing 4-18.

***Listing 4-18.*** Adding form submission logic

```
import { SubmitHandler } from "react-hook-form";

export default function Signup() {

    const onSubmit: SubmitHandler<FormData> = (data) => {
    fetch("/signup", {
      method: "post",
      body: JSON.stringify(data),
    });
  };

  return (
    <form onSubmit={handleSubmit(onSubmit)}>
```

Now I would like to add some features to the submit button as described initially. For that I would get the isDirty and isSubmitting values from formState as can be seen in Listing 4-19.

***Listing 4-19.*** Extracting isDirty and isSubmitting from formState

```
const {
    register,
    handleSubmit,
    formState: { errors, isDirty, isSubmitting },
  } = useForm<FormData>();
```

Using these values, I will disable the submit button if isDirty is false or if isSubmitting is true. Also, I will change the submit button text from Signup to Submitting … if isSubmitting is true as can be seen in Listing 4-20.

***Listing 4-20.*** Using isDirty and isSubmitting

```
<button type="submit" disabled={!isDirty || isSubmitting}>
  {isSubmitting ? "Submitting..." : "Signup"}
</button>
```

In order to see the isSubmitting in action, I will add a dummy delay in the onSubmit function of 1 s as can be seen in Listing 4-21.

***Listing 4-21.*** Adding a dummy delay in the onSubmit function

```
const sleep = (timeout: number) =>
  new Promise((resolve) => {
    setTimeout(resolve, timeout);
  });

  const onSubmit: SubmitHandler<FormData> = async (data) => {
    await sleep(1000);
    fetch("/signup", {
      method: "post",
      body: JSON.stringify(data),
    });
  };
```

Now you will be able to see the isSubmitting effect in action. The button would be disabled initially when no field would be modified. During submission the text of the submit button would change from Signup to Submitting ..., and it would be disabled to avoid multiple submissions.

# Integrating Controlled Components

Usually when frontend developers work on the UI, they don't make their components themselves; they use UI components from third-party libraries like Material UI and others.

However, these libraries mostly have controlled components, and you know that React Hook Form works in an uncontrolled manner. In order to integrate controlled components (made by you or a third party), you will need to use React Hook Form's Controller interface.

I will import the Controller component from React Hook Form. Then I will use that component instead of our usual input field.

The main prop of this component is the control prop, which I will get from the useForm hook. In the name prop, the field key would go. I can pass the register options in the rules prop of the Controller component. Finally in the render prop, I will render the controlled TextField component I would get from Material UI.

For demonstration I will use this Controller component in place of the first name input field as can be seen in Listing 4-22. The same principle would be used for other instances as well where applicable.

***Listing 4-22.*** Integrating controlled components in React Hook Form

```
import { Controller, SubmitHandler, useForm } from "react-
hook-form";
import { TextField } from "@mui/material";

export default function Signup() {
const {
    register,
    handleSubmit,
    control,
    formState: { errors, isValid, isDirty, isSubmitting },
  } = useForm<FormData>();

  return (
    <form onSubmit={handleSubmit(onSubmit)}>
      <div className="form-container">
```

```
<div>
  <Controller
    name="firstName"
    control={control}
    rules={{ required: true }}
    render={({ field }) => (
      <TextField
        style={{ marginBottom: 10 }}
        label="First name"
        variant="outlined"
        {...field}
      />
    )}
  />
  {errors.firstName?.type === "required" && (
    <p className="error">First Name is required</p>
  )}
</div>
```

The form after replacing the first name input field with Material UI's TextField would look like Figure 4-4.

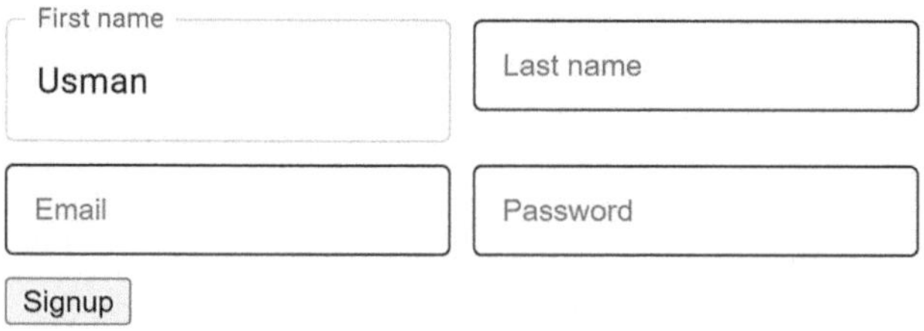

***Figure 4-4.*** *Material UI TextField component integration*

# Summary

In this chapter, I built two forms using React Hook Form, one BMI calculator and one Signup form. You saw how we could, using details regarding a form, build that form with validations and a lot of other custom functionalities.

In the next chapter, I will take a deep dive into validations using React Hook Form.

# CHAPTER 5

# Validation

In the last chapter, I made two forms using React Hook Form, a BMI calculator and a Signup form. During this process, you learned how to integrate state with input fields, how to add basic validations, how to add custom features like disabling the submit button when the form is submitting, and finally how to integrate controlled components with React Hook Form.

In this chapter, I will discuss validation in detail. I will demonstrate how you can validate or revalidate forms at particular intervals (change, blur, submit). I will also demonstrate how you can integrate third-party schema solutions like Yup and Zod to validate your forms.

For styling, I will use the same stylesheet we used for the Signup form in Chapter 4 since we will be using the same form for understanding different validation patterns in this chapter. I will name this stylesheet `Validation.css` and will be using it throughout this chapter.

## Using register Options

In the previous chapter, I used the register options in the `register` function to apply some validation rules on input fields like required, pattern matching, minimum length, etc.

In this section, I will apply the same rules again but using a slightly different approach so that you can know all the ways in which you can do validation using register options.

© Usman Abdur Rehman 2025
U. A. Rehman, *Web Forms with React*, Apress Pocket Guides,
https://doi.org/10.1007/979-8-8688-1224-8_5

# register with Validation and Error Message

In the previous chapter, I defined validation rules in the `register` function in such a way that I passed the validation criteria directly as a value to the register options object properties like the following.

***Listing 5-1.*** Validation using register options

```
<input
  {...register("email", {
    required: true,
    pattern: /^[\w-\.]+@([\w-]+\.)+[\w-]{2,4}$/,
  })}
  placeholder="Email"
/>
```

In order to show error messages, I checked if the `type` property of the error object is `required`, `pattern`, or something else, and based on that I mapped the errors as can be seen in Listing 5-2.

***Listing 5-2.*** Mapping errors

```
{errors.email?.type === "required" && (
  <p className="error">Email is required</p>
)}
{errors.email?.type === "pattern" && (
  <p className="error">Email is invalid</p>
)}
```

Another way to do it is to specify the error message inside the register options so that it can be used directly like `errors?.email?.message`.

For required validation only, you would specify the error message as a value to the `required` property of register options. For other validation options, you can assign an object as a value, which would be of the following shape as can be seen in Listing 5-3.

***Listing 5-3.*** Shape of the register options validation object

```
{
  value: any;
  message: string;
}
```

The validation criteria value (e.g., /^[\w-\.]+@([\w-]+\.)+[\w-]{2,4}$/ in the case of pattern in Listing 5-1) would go in the value property, and the error message would go in the message property. After making these changes, the validations for the email field would look like the following as can be seen in Listing 5-4.

***Listing 5-4.*** Validation using register options with a validation message

```
<div>
        <input
          {...register("email", {
            required: "Email is required",
            pattern: {
              value: /^[\w-\.]+@([\w-]+\.)+[\w-]{2,4}$/,
              message: "Email is invalid",
            },
          })}
          placeholder="Email"
        />
        <p className="error">{errors?.email?.message}</p>
      </div>
```

The same principle would be applied for other validations like minLength in the password field. minLength would receive an object as a value where the value property would have the value 10 and the message property would have the corresponding error message.

# register with the validate Function

Using the predefined register options described above (`required`, `pattern`, `minLength`), you can do basic validations like checking if a value is present, pattern matching, etc. However, if you want to do complex validations without using any third-party library like Zod, you can make use of the `validate` function.

The `validate` property in register options can accept a function or an object with functions as values as can be seen in Listing 5-5.

***Listing 5-5.*** Types of values the validate property in register options can take

```
{
  // function
  validate: () => {},

  // object of functions
  validate: {
    key1: () => {},
    key2: () => {},
  },
};
```

If I just specify a function as a value to the `validate` property, then I can only add one validation in this function. If this function returns `true`, then that means that validation has passed, and it shouldn't show any error. Otherwise, I have to return a string, which would be the validation error. I can redo the email pattern matching validation using the `validate` function as can be seen in Listing 5-6.

***Listing 5-6.*** validate property with a function value

```
<input
          {...register("email", {
            required: "Email is required",
            validate: (email) => {
              if (/^[\w-\.]+@([\w-]+\.)+[\w-]{2,4}$/.
              test(email)) {
                return true;
              }
              return "Email is invalid";
            },
          })}
          placeholder="Email"
        />
```

I used the regex's `test` function in JavaScript to test if the email value in the input matches that particular regex pattern. If that was the case, I returned `true`; otherwise, I returned the error string.

The `validate` function can also be async. Let's say I want to check, by sending a call to a backend, if the email entered is valid or not. I can do that by making `validate` an `async` function as can be seen in Listing 5-7.

***Listing 5-7.*** validate property with an async function value

```
<input
          {...register("email", {
            required: "Email is required",
            validate: async (email) => {
              const isValid = await (
                await fetch(`/isValidEmail?email=${email}`)
              ).json();
              return isValid || "Email is invalid";
```

```
        },
    })}
    placeholder="Email"
/>
```

If I want to add multiple validations to an input in the `validate` function as the case for the email input field (required and pattern matching), I can pass an object in the `validate` property, as can be seen in Listing 5-8, that expects a string key that would be used as the error type and a function value that works the exact same way as shown before.

***Listing 5-8.*** validate property with an object of functions value

```
<input
        {...register("email", {
          validate: {
            isRequired: (email) => {
              return !!email || "Email is required";
            },
            isEmailValid: (email) => {
              if (/^[\w-\.]+@([\w-]+\.)+[\w-]{2,4}$/.
              test(email)) {
                return true;
              }
              return "Email is invalid";
            },
          },
        })}
        placeholder="Email"
    />
```

Using this syntax, I was able to combine both validations, required and pattern matching, in one `validate` object.

However, you saw that up until now I was only able to show one validation error at a time. Sometimes you would want to show multiple validation errors at once for a field. I will take a look at it in the next section.

# Validation Options

There are a lot of validation options that can be passed to the useForm hook to change how validation is applied to the form fields. In this section, I will cover those options.

## mode/reValidateMode

Validation in React Hook Form is divided into two categories, validation and revalidation. The validation that happens before the first form submission is just called validation, while the validation that happens after the first form submission is called revalidation.

Using the mode and reValidateMode params in the useForm hook, you can change the validation strategy before and after form submission (for validation and revalidation). By default, validation would be triggered on the submit event, and revalidation would happen on change events.

The mode param can have any of the values shown in Listing 5-9. The default value for the mode param is onSubmit.

***Listing 5-9.*** Type for the mode param

```
onChange | onBlur | onSubmit | onTouched | all
```

Based on what value you pass to the mode param, the validation would be triggered at different stages of the form cycle. Table 5-1 would help you understand that.

**Table 5-1.** *Value Descriptions for the mode Param*

| Name | Description |
|---|---|
| onSubmit | Validation is triggered on the submit event. |
| onBlur | Validation is triggered on the blur event. |
| onChange | Validation is triggered on the change event. |
| onTouched | Validation is initially triggered on the first blur event. After that, it is triggered on every change event. |
| all | Validation is triggered on both blur and change events. |

The reValidateMode param can have any of the values shown in Listing 5-10. The default value for the reValidateMode param is onChange.

**Listing 5-10.** Type for the reValidateMode param

```
onChange I onBlur I onSubmit
```

Based on what value you pass to the reValidateMode param, the validation would be triggered at different stages of the form cycle. Table 5-2 will help you understand that.

**Table 5-2.** *Value Descriptions for the reValidateMode Param*

| Name | Description |
|---|---|
| onSubmit | Validation is triggered on the submit event. |
| onBlur | Validation is triggered on the blur event. |
| onChange | Validation is triggered on the change event. |

You can choose a combination of these params based on what your form needs. If you value performance more, then maybe try to trigger validations on blur and submit events. If you constantly want to perform validation on every keystroke (change event) because that is what your form demands, then you can trigger validation on the change event. And so on …

For a small form, the default values for these params are okay. However, for larger forms, I would advise you to choose onBlur for the reValidateMode param so that revalidation only occurs on blur events.

## criteriaMode

For the validation examples I have shown you, the errors object only contains one error even if multiple validation errors are present for an input. This can be controlled via the criteriaMode param.

The default value of criteriaMode param is firstError. This means that React Hook Form would only return the first error based on its validation order (random). If you want to change this behavior and want all errors to be returned, then you would change its value to all.

When the criteriaMode param value is all, another property, types, would be added to the corresponding field error object, which would have the following shape as can be seen in Listing 5-11.

*Listing 5-11.* The shape for the types property inside the errors object

```
{
  type: string;
  ref: HTMLInputElement;
  message: string;
  types:{
```

```
    [errorKey: string]: string
  };
}
```

where the key would be a predefined error key like `required` and `minLength` in case you are using those to add validations or the key in the `validate` object if you are using the `validate` object for adding validations. The `value` would be the error string you would specify in the corresponding validation.

If now I want to show all the current errors of a field, for example, the email field, it would look like the following as can be seen in Listing 5-12.

***Listing 5-12.*** Mapping errors using the types property

```
{/* Map errors in random order */}
    {Object.values(errors?.email?.types || {})?.
    map((error) => (
      <p className="error">{error}</p>
    ))}

{/* Map errors in order of your choice */}
    {[
      errors?.email?.types?.isRequired,
      errors?.email?.types?.isEmailValid,
    ].map((error) => (
      <p className="error">{error}</p>
    ))}
```

As you can see in this example, if you don't care about the order in which validation errors are shown, you can just map over them using `Object.values`. However, if you do care about the order, then you can create an array of errors yourself with your specified order and then map that.

## shouldFocusError

This param is true by default. If this param is true, upon form submission, the first field that has a validation error would be focused, which is a good UX. However, if you want to disable this behavior, you can pass false in this param.

## delayError

If you want that the errors are not displayed instantly when validation happens, then you can pass the number of milliseconds by which you want the error display to be delayed in this param.

# Validation Using Schema

Validation can also be done by passing a schema defined using a third-party library like Yup, Zod, Joi, etc. This is usually the preferred approach to do validation as well, if you are already using Yup, Zod, etc., in your project to validate something else. Using a schema to do validation would make sure there is a standard approach being used to do validation. Let's see how you can integrate these libraries with React Hook Form.

First of all, in order to use schema validation, I would have to install a package @hookform/resolvers using the installation command in Listing 5-13.

*Listing 5-13.* Installation command for the @hookform/ resolvers library

```
npm install @hookform/resolvers
```

After that I will import the resolver function for the corresponding schema library from this package. I would use this to create a resolver from the schema generated from the third-party library and pass it in the resolver param of the useForm hook.

In this section, I will only discuss Yup and Zod, Yup because Yup is already used as a schema validation library for Formik and Zod because it is the most popular schema validation library. Now I will take the Signup form from the last chapter and implement validation for that form using Yup and Zod.

## Schema Validation Using Yup

First of all, I will import the yupResolver as discussed before. Then I will create the schema using Yup, pass that schema in the yupResolver function, and then pass the result into the resolver property of the useForm hook as can be seen in Listing 5-14.

***Listing 5-14.*** Schema validation using Yup

```
import { SubmitHandler, useForm } from "react-hook-form";
import { yupResolver } from "@hookform/resolvers/yup";
import * as yup from "yup";
import "./Validation.css";

interface FormData {
  firstName: string;
  lastName?: string;
  password: string;
  email: string;
}
const schema = yup.object().shape({
  firstName: yup.string().required("First Name is required"),
  email: yup.string().email("Email is
 invalid").required("Email is required"),
  password: yup
    .string()
```

```
    .required("Password is required")
    .min(10, "Password should have at least 10 characters"),
});

export default function Signup() {
  const {
    register,
    handleSubmit,
    formState: { errors },
  } = useForm<FormData>({
    criteriaMode: "all",
    resolver: yupResolver(schema),
  });

  const onSubmit: SubmitHandler<FormData> = async () => {};

  return (
    <form onSubmit={handleSubmit(onSubmit)}>
      <div className="form-container">
        <div>
          <input {...register("firstName")} placeholder="First
          name" />
          {Object.values(errors?.firstName?.types || {})?.
          map((error) => (
            <p className="error">{error}</p>
          ))}
        </div>
        <div>
          <input {...register("lastName")} placeholder="Last
          name" />
        </div>
        <div>
```

```
        <input {...register("email")} placeholder="Email" />
        {Object.values(errors?.email?.types || {})?.
        map((error) => (
          <p className="error">{error}</p>
        ))}
      </div>
      <div>
        <input {...register("password")}
        placeholder="Password" />
        {Object.values(errors?.password?.types || {})?.
        map((error) => (
          <p className="error">{error}</p>
        ))}
      </div>
    </div>

    <button type="submit">Signup</button>
  </form>
  );
}
```

## Schema Validation Using Zod

I will do the same thing for Zod where I will create the schema using Zod, pass that schema in the zodResolver function, and then pass the result into the resolver property of the useForm hook as can be seen in Listing 5-15.

*Listing 5-15.* Schema validation using Zod

```
import { zodResolver } from "@hookform/resolvers/zod";
import { z } from "zod";
```

```
const schema = z.object({
  firstName: z.string().min(1, { message: "First Name is
  required" }),
  email: z
    .string()
    .min(1, { message: "Email is required" })
    .email("Email is invalid"),
  password: z.string().min(10, "Password should have at least
  10 characters"),
});

const {
    register,
    handleSubmit,
    formState: { errors },
  } = useForm<FormData>({
    criteriaMode: "all",
    resolver: zodResolver(schema),
  });
```

# Summary

In this section, we looked at validations in detail. I explained how you can display custom validation messages, make custom validation functions using the validate register option, change validation strategies using various useForm params, and at the end perform validations using third-party libraries like Zod and Yup.

In the next chapter, I will demonstrate how you can implement some common form scenarios using React Hook Form.

# CHAPTER 6

# Common Use Cases

In the last chapter, I discussed validation in detail. I discussed how custom error messages can be added in register options for validations, the `validate` function, the `useForm` hook params related to validation, and how third-party schema validation libraries like Zod and Yup can be integrated with React Hook Form for validation.

In this chapter, I will discuss some common form use cases like reusable fields, nested forms, etc. and how they can be implemented using React Hook Form.

For some form examples I will discuss in this chapter, I will be using a minimal stylesheet, which is given below in Listing 6-1. I will reference this in the code examples as `Form.css` wherever I will use it.

***Listing 6-1.*** CSS styles for form scenario examples

```
* {
  box-sizing: border-box;
}

form {
  width: 200px;
}

select,
input[type="text"] {
  padding: 12px;
```

```css
  margin-bottom: 10px;
  border-radius: 4px;
  border: 1px solid black;
  display: block;
  width: 100%;
}

label {
  font-size: 14px;
}

input[type="checkbox"] {
  margin-bottom: 10px;
}

.error {
  margin: 0;
  margin-bottom: 10px;
  color: red;
  font-size: 14px;
}

.name-list-item {
  display: flex;
  gap: 6px;
  margin-bottom: 10px;
}

.name-list-item > input {
  margin: 0;
  width: 140px;
}
```

# Deeply Nested Form

For smaller forms, if some field needs to use some method or state from the useForm hook, that field can get it directly from the useForm hook via props. However, for larger forms with deeply nested fields and sub-forms, you would need to do prop drilling to get the props everywhere, which is not a recommended approach in React.

In cases like these, it is better to use React Hook Form's FormProvider component. The FormProvider component uses React's Context API under the hood to provide all form-related methods and data to every child component of the FormProvider. If you want to get any form method or state in any child component of the FormProvider, you can get it using the useFormContext hook. Its usage would look like the following.

***Listing 6-2.*** Example of a deeply nested form using FormProvider/ useFormContext

```
import { useForm, FormProvider, useFormContext } from "react-
hook-form";
import "./Form.css";

interface FormData {
  name: string;
}

const NestedInput = () => {
  const {
    register,
    formState: { errors },
  } = useFormContext<FormData>();

  return (
    <div>
      <input
```

```
      {...register("name", { required: "Name is required" })}
      type="text"
      placeholder="Name"
    />
    <p className="error">{errors.name?.message}</p>
  </div>
 );
};

export default function NestedForm() {
  const form = useForm<FormData>();
  const { handleSubmit } = form;

  const onSubmit = () => {};

  return (
    <FormProvider {...form}>
      <form onSubmit={handleSubmit(onSubmit)}>
        <NestedInput />
        <button type="submit">Signup</button>
      </form>
    </FormProvider>
  );
}
```

As you can see in Listing 6-2, NestedInput is a child of the FormProvider component, and I was able to use the form methods and state like register and errors inside the NestedInput without any need for prop drilling from the parent to the child via the useFormContext hook. This method can be very useful for creating reusable fields, which I will be taking a look at in a later section.

# Dependent Fields

In a previous chapter, I discussed the watch function. The watch function can be used to watch for changes in any field. But the downside of this is that the whole form will rerender whenever a particular field would change.

If you want that only a particular child component (an isolated dependent field component) should rerender on some field change, then you can use the useWatch hook.

The useWatch hook expects certain params, the most important of which is name.

You can pass either a string or an array of strings (which corresponds to field keys in the form) to the name param. Another param is the control param. If you are using the FormProvider component, you don't need to pass this control in the useWatch hook; otherwise, you will have to pass the control you get from the useForm hook in the control param of the useWatch hook.

In this example as can be seen in Listing 6-3, I have three fields, a text field Name, a checkbox Is graduated?, and a specializations select field. I only want to show the specializations select field if the Is graduated? checkbox is checked. I can do that by extracting the specializations select field (the dependent field) into a separate component and then, using the useWatch hook, rendering that component if the particular checkbox is checked (its corresponding value is true). Otherwise, I can return null. It would look something like the following.

***Listing 6-3.*** Example of dependent fields using useWatch

```
import {
  FormProvider,
  SubmitHandler,
  useForm,
```

```
  useFormContext,
  useWatch,
} from "react-hook-form";
import "./Form.css";

interface FormData {
  name: string;
  isGraduated: boolean;
  specialization: string;
}

const SPECIALIZATIONS = ["Electrical", "Software", "Data
Science"];

const SpecializationField = () => {
  const isGraduated = useWatch({ name: "isGraduated" });
  const { register } = useFormContext<FormData>();
  if (!isGraduated) return null;

  return (
    <select {...register("specialization")}>
      {SPECIALIZATIONS.map((specialization) => (
        <option value={specialization}>{specialization}
        </option>
      ))}
    </select>
  );
};

export default function DependentFields() {
  const form = useForm<FormData>();
  const { register, handleSubmit } = form;
  const onSubmit: SubmitHandler<FormData> = async (data) => {};
```

```
return (
  <FormProvider {...form}>
    <form onSubmit={handleSubmit(onSubmit)}>
      <input {...register("name")} placeholder="Name"
      type="text" />

      <div>
        <label>
          <input {...register("isGraduated")}
          type="checkbox" />
          Is Graduated?
        </label>
      </div>

      <SpecializationField />
      <button type="submit">Submit</button>
    </form>
  </FormProvider>
);
}
```

As you can see in the SpecializationField component, I have passed
the field key of the checkbox, isGraduated, in the useWatch hook, which
gives me the value of that checkbox. If it is false, then I return null,
which means nothing would be rendered; otherwise, I would render
the specializations select field. If you would put a console.log on the
DependentFields component as well as in the SpecializationField
component, you will see that whenever the Is graduated? checkbox would
change, only the SpecializationField component would rerender,
not the whole form, which is a very performant approach for making
dependent fields.

# Reusable Fields

In any application, there are a lot of fields/sub-forms and so on, which are reusable across many forms, for example, the email and password fields. For a general website, the email and password fields are present in the Signin form, Signup form, Edit Profile form, etc. These two fields along with their respective code regarding the register function and validations can be made into a separate component known as `Credentials,` which can then be reused in any form like Signin, Signup, etc. I will make use of the `FormProvider` component so that I can extract the `register` function and necessary logic right there in the `Credentials` component using the `useFormContext` hook and the component doesn't require any props for its usage. It would look something like the following.

***Listing 6-4.*** Example of reusable fields/forms using FormProvider/useFormContext

```
import {
  FormProvider,
  SubmitHandler,
  useForm,
  useFormContext,
} from "react-hook-form";
import "./Form.css";

interface UserFormData {
  firstName: string;
  lastName: string;
  bio: string;
  age: number;
  email: string;
  password: string;
}
```

```
const Credentials = () => {
  const {
    register,
    formState: { errors },
  } = useFormContext<UserFormData>();

  return (
    <>
      <div>
        <input
          {...register("email", {
            required: true,
            pattern: /^[\w-\.]+@([\w-]+\.)+[\w-]{2,4}$/,
          })}
          placeholder="Email"
          type="text"
        />
        {errors.email?.type === "required" && (
          <p className="error">Email is required</p>
        )}
        {errors.email?.type === "pattern" && (
          <p className="error">Email is invalid</p>
        )}
      </div>
      <div>
        <input
          {...register("password", {
            required: true,
            minLength: 10,
          })}
          placeholder="Password"
          type="text"
```

```
          />
          {errors.password?.type === "required" && (
            <p className="error">Password is required</p>
          )}
          {errors.password?.type === "minLength" && (
            <p className="error">Password should have at least 10
            characters</p>
          )}
        </div>
      </>
    );
  };

export function ReusableSignup() {
  const form = useForm<UserFormData>();
  const { register, handleSubmit } = form;
  const onSubmit: SubmitHandler<UserFormData> = async
  (data) => {};

  return (
    <FormProvider {...form}>
      <form onSubmit={handleSubmit(onSubmit)}>
        <input
          {...register("firstName")}
          placeholder="First Name"
          type="text"
        />
        <input {...register("lastName")} placeholder="Last
        Name" type="text" />

        <Credentials />
        <button type="submit">Submit</button>
      </form>
```

```
        </FormProvider>
    );
}

export function ReusableSignin() {
    const form = useForm<UserFormData>();
    const { handleSubmit } = form;
const onSubmit: SubmitHandler<UserFormData> = async
(data) => {};

    return (
        <FormProvider {...form}>
            <form onSubmit={handleSubmit(onSubmit)}>
                <Credentials />
                <button type="submit">Submit</button>
            </form>
        </FormProvider>
    );
}

export function ReusableProfile() {
    const form = useForm<UserFormData>();
    const { register, handleSubmit } = form;
 const onSubmit: SubmitHandler<UserFormData> = async
 (data) => {};

    return (
        <FormProvider {...form}>
            <form onSubmit={handleSubmit(onSubmit)}>
                <input
                    {...register("firstName")}
                    placeholder="First Name"
                    type="text"
```

```
    />
    <input {...register("lastName")} placeholder="Last
    Name" type="text" />

    <Credentials />

    <textarea {...register("bio")} placeholder="Bio" />
    <input
      {...register("age", { valueAsNumber: true })}
      placeholder="Age"
      type="number"
    />
    <button type="submit">Submit</button>
  </form>
</FormProvider>
);
}
```

As you can see in Listing 6-4, I utilized the same principle I used in the nested form example where I created a component Credentials where I got the form-related accessories from the useFormContext hook and I reused these fields very easily without the need to pass any props in three forms (Signin, Signup, and Edit Profile) by wrapping them up in the FormProvider component.

If you want to use any component from this example, you can import them using named imports like import {ReusableProfile} from … since I haven't used any default export in this example.

# Reusable Controlled Components

In a previous chapter, I talked about how you need to use the Controller interface to integrate controlled components with React Hook Form since React Hook Form works in an uncontrolled manner because of the use of refs.

However, a lot of repetition of code occurs while integrating controlled components where every controlled component in the form needs to be wrapped by the Controller component. A better approach is to extract these controlled components into separate components where they can get the field-related methods and data using the useController hook.

The useController hook just like the useWatch hook would get the control automatically via context if FormProvider is being used; otherwise, it has to be passed manually via props. All the other params to this hook are the same as the Controller component discussed previously (name, rules, etc.). I will make a reusable component (as can be seen in Listing 6-5) for the Material UI's TextField component using the useController hook and then use it just like I would use a normal HTML input like the following.

***Listing 6-5.*** Example of reusable controlled components using useController

```
import { TextField } from "@mui/material";
import {
  FormProvider,
  RegisterOptions,
  SubmitHandler,
  useController,
  useForm,
} from "react-hook-form";

interface FormData {
  name: string;
}

const Input = ({
  name,
  rules,
  label,
```

```
}: {
  name: string;
  rules?: RegisterOptions;
  label?: string;
}) => {
  const { field } = useController({
    name,
    rules,
  });

  return (
    <TextField
      {...field}
      inputRef={field.ref}
      style={{ marginBottom: 10 }}
      label={label}
    />
  );
};

export const ReusableControlledForm = () => {
  const form = useForm<FormData>();
  const {
    handleSubmit,
    formState: { errors },
  } = form;

  const onSubmit: SubmitHandler<FormData> = async (data)
  =>   {};

  return (
    <FormProvider {...form}>
      <form onSubmit={handleSubmit(onSubmit)}>
```

```
    <Input name="name" label="Name" rules={{ required:
    true }} />
    {errors.name && <p>Name is required</p>}
    <div />
    <button type="submit">Submit</button>
    </form>
  </FormProvider>
  );
};
```

# Mapping Multiple Fields

Oftentimes you need to map multiple fields of a similar type in your form. It is essential that there is a standard approach for mutating the array state for the fields data, for example, appending, removing, updating, replacing fields, etc. from the field list.

React Hook Form provides a hook useFieldArray for that particular purpose. useFieldArray expects a control param if the form isn't wrapped with FormProvider; otherwise, it gets it from the form context. It also expects a name param, which should match a field key. It returns a fields variable, which is an array you can map to render the fields + a plethora of array functions like append, remove, etc., which can be used to perform mutation operations on the array state easily.

Let's say I have a form in which I have to enter the names of users in the form of a list. For that purpose, I will map a series of fields comprising of a text input and a delete button, which can be used to remove the corresponding field from the list.

This implementation using the useFieldArray hook would look like the following.

***Listing 6-6.*** Example of mapping multiple fields using useFieldArray

```
import { useForm, useFieldArray, SubmitHandler } from "react-
hook-form";
import "./Form.css";

interface FormData {
  users: { name: string }[];
}

export default function MultipleFields() {
  const { register, control, handleSubmit } =
  useForm<FormData>({
    defaultValues: { users: [{ name: "Usman" }] },
  });
  const { fields, append, remove, replace, insert, swap,
  prepend } =
    useFieldArray({
      control,
      name: "users",
    });

  const onSubmit: SubmitHandler<FormData> = (data) => {};

  return (
    <form onSubmit={handleSubmit(onSubmit)}>
      <div>
        {fields.map((item, index) => (
          <div key={item.id} className="name-list-item">
            <input {...register(`users.${index}.name`)}
            type="text" />
```

```
    <button type="button" onClick={() =>
    remove(index)}>
      Delete
    </button>
  </div>
 ))}
</div>
<button type="button" onClick={() => append({
name: "" })}>
  Add new user
</button>
</form>
);
}
```

As you can see in Listing 6-6, I mapped the fields using the fields variable I got from the useFieldArray hook. Every object in the fields array will have an id that would uniquely distinguish each field. This id would be generated by the useFieldArray hook. This id would be used as a key for each field. The index would be used to create the field key for the register function for each field.

I also used the append and remove functions I got from the hook to add and remove fields from the field list. The append method expects an object of the type of the field specified in the FormData type (type passed in the useForm hook). Calling the append method would add that object to the corresponding field array state. The remove function expects a number param that corresponds to the index of the item you want to be removed from the field list.

Similarly, there are a lot of other array functions that you get from the useFieldArray hook like replace, insert, swap, etc., and you can use them to perform array operations easily without the need of manually mutating state.

As the `MultipleFields` function in this example is a default exported function, in order to render this component in another component, you will use a default import like `import MultipleFields from ...` to import it.

# Summary

In this chapter, I looked at some common form scenarios that developers face while working on forms from reusable fields to nested forms, dependent fields, mapping of multiple fields, etc. I then showed you how React Hook Form makes it very convenient to work with these scenarios.

And that is it for this book. I hope this book helped you level up your forms skills in React. I wish you the best of luck in your frontend career.

# Index

## A

async function, 23, 49

## B

BMI calculator
    CSS styles, 27
    error object, 30
    form, 27, 28
    HTML skeleton, 26
    HTML structure, 26
    onSubmit function, 31
    react component, 26
    register function, 29
    required property, 29
    salient features, 25
    type property, 30
    useForm hook, 28
    valueAsNumber:true, 29
    values, 32

## C

Common form use cases
    CSS styles, 61
    deeply nested form, 63, 64
    dependent fields, 65–67

    mapping multiple fields, 75–78
    reusable controlled
        components, 72, 73, 75
    reusable fields, 68–72
Controlled components
    integrating, 41–43
    reusable, 72–75
Credentials component, 68
criteriaMode param, 53, 54
Cross-platform, 13

## D

Deeply nested form, 63–64
defaultValues param, 22, 23
delayError param, 55
DependentFields component, 67
dev tools, 14, 16

## E

Email regex, 37

## F

Form builder, 15, 16
Formik, 7–10, 12, 15–17, 22, 56